Easy
HOLIDAY
Entertaining

Published by Barbour Publishing, Inc., P.O. Box 719, Uhrichsville, Ohio 44683, www.barbourbooks.com

Our mission is to publish and distribute inspirational products offering exceptional value and biblical encouragement to the masses.

Member of the
Evangelical Christian
Publishers Association

Printed in China.

Easy
HOLIDAY
Entertaining

Recipes & Inspiration to Make the Season Merry

BARBOUR
PUBLISHING

Welcome to *Easy Holiday Entertaining*! Here you'll find a plethora of tasty recipes, festive inspiration, and ideas to make your holiday get-togethers truly merry and bright. Each page is a stand-alone recipe card that can be easily removed from the book to add to your collection of other holiday treats; or you may choose to share some of the cards with friends and family. Consider creating the dish to give as a gift and attaching the recipe card with a bright ribbon. Or maybe slip a recipe card or two into your Christmas cards this year. You may also wish to keep the book as a whole—no matter how you use it, you can't go wrong!

Recipes are organized in colorful sections:

Breakfasts

Main and Side Dishes

Desserts

Appetizers

Make Yourself at Home: Tips and Tricks for the Hostess

Breakfasts

Entertaining 101:

- The first rule of simple entertaining is to have fun. If you, the host, are enjoying yourself, others will, too. Let your hair down and be real. Be rested and ready, happy to see your friends. Make them know how glad you are to be spending Christmastime with them.

- Plan a simple protein-rich breakfast for overnight guests in your home. Also have cereal available and a toaster out for those who just want a piece of toast to start the day.

- Always wash and dry new stiff, scratchy sheets and towels at least three times before using them for sleepover company. This makes them soft and absorbent.

- When entertaining overnight guests, prepare messy breakfast meats in advance. Frying and cleanup can be done days ahead, meat stored in the refrigerator and popped into the microwave for a minute to reheat and crisp up.

> In Bethlehem is born the Holy Child. . .
> O, my heart is full of mirth at Jesus' birth.
> GEORGE FRIDERIC HANDEL

> *Lo, this is our God; we have waited for him. . .*
> *we will be glad and rejoice in his salvation.*
> ISAIAH 25:9

Escalloped Apples

The aroma that fills your home as these apples bake will draw everyone to the kitchen to see what's baking. They are wonderful on their own or paired as a topping over pancakes or baked oatmeal.

6 apples, peeled, cored and, sliced
½ cup sugar
3 tablespoons flour
½ teaspoon cinnamon
½ teaspoon nutmeg

¼ teaspoon cloves
½ cup raisins
½ cup walnuts, chopped
1 teaspoon vanilla
½ cup whole milk

Place apples in large bowl. In small bowl, mix together sugar, flour, cinnamon, nutmeg, and cloves. Stir spice mixture into apples until evenly distributed.

Fold in raisins and walnuts. Spoon into greased 2-quart casserole dish. Mix vanilla and milk; pour evenly over apple mixture. Bake at 350 degrees for 45 to 60 minutes, or until soft and bubbly. Allow to cool slightly before serving.

Notes

....

....

....

....

....

Crab and Spinach Quiche

For a special holiday breakfast or brunch, this quiche uses seafood instead of the traditional ham or bacon. Fresh fruit and muffins make good accompaniments for breakfast.

5 eggs
1½ cups half-and-half
¼ teaspoon salt
⅛ teaspoon pepper
⅛ teaspoon nutmeg
⅛ teaspoon hot sauce
1 cup swiss cheese, shredded
1½ cups parmesan cheese, grated

3 tablespoons flour
6 to 8 ounces canned or frozen crabmeat, thawed, drained, and flaked
1 (10 ounce) package frozen chopped spinach, thawed and well drained
2 (9 inch) pastry-lined pie plates or quiche pans

In a large bowl, lightly beat eggs. Add half-and-half, salt, pepper, nutmeg, and hot sauce; set aside. Combine cheeses and flour; add to egg mixture with the crab and spinach. Mix well. Pour into two 9-inch, pastry-lined pie plates or quiche pans. Bake at 350 degrees for 50 minutes or until a knife inserted near center comes out clean. Let set 5 minutes before cutting. Cut into wedges.

Notes

Cherry Strata

BREAD MIXTURE:

12 cups day-old italian bread cubes
(½-inch cubes)
1 (8 ounce) package cream cheese
½ cup sugar, divided
½ teaspoon almond extract

½ cup dried cherries or cranberries
½ cup pecans, chopped
4 eggs
1½ cups half-and-half
1 teaspoon cinnamon

CHERRY SYRUP:

1 (14½ ounce) can sour cherries, chopped
1 cup sugar

1 cup corn syrup
½ teaspoon almond extract

BREAD MIXTURE: Place 8 cups of bread cubes in greased 9x13-inch baking
pan. In mixing bowl, beat cream cheese until smooth; add ¼ cup sugar and

almond extract. Beat until well mixed. Stir in cherries and pecans: spoon over bread. Top with remaining bread cubes. In bowl, whisk eggs, half-and-half, cinnamon, and remaining sugar; pour over bread. Bake uncovered at 350 degrees for 35 to 40 minutes or until browned. Let stand 5 minutes before serving. CHERRY SYRUP: Combine cherries, sugar, and corn syrup in saucepan; bring to a boil. Reduce heat; simmer for 15 minutes. Remove from heat; stir in extract. Serve warm over strata.

Notes

....

....

....

Pumpkin Pancakes with Cinnamon Syrup

SYRUP:
½ cup sugar
½ cup brown sugar
2 tablespoons cornstarch

½ teaspoon cinnamon
1 teaspoon vanilla
1 cup water

PANCAKES:
2 cups flour
3 tablespoons brown sugar
2 teaspoons baking powder
1 teaspoon baking soda
1 teaspoon allspice
1 teaspoon cinnamon
½ teaspoon ginger

½ teaspoon salt
1½ cups milk
1 cup pumpkin puree
1 egg
2 tablespoons vegetable oil
2 tablespoons vinegar

SYRUP: In small saucepan, mix together the sugar, brown sugar, cornstarch, and cinnamon. Stir in vanilla and water. Bring to rolling boil, stirring often. Continue to boil and stir until mixture thickens to syrup consistency. Remove from heat; cool 10 minutes before serving. PANCAKES: In mixing bowl, combine flour, brown sugar, baking powder, baking soda, allspice, cinnamon, ginger, and salt. In a separate bowl, mix together milk, pumpkin, egg, oil, and vinegar. Stir flour mixture into pumpkin mixture, just until blended. Let batter sit about 10 minutes, until it becomes bubbly. Heat a lightly oiled griddle or frying pan over medium-high heat. Scoop approximately ¼ cup batter onto griddle. Spread the batter out a little bit to make thinner pancakes. Brown on both sides and serve hot with cinnamon syrup.

Cranberry Cream Coffee Cake

CAKE:
2 cups flour
1 cup sugar
1½ teaspoons baking powder
½ teaspoon baking soda
1 egg
¾ cup orange juice

¼ cup butter
1 teaspoon vanilla
2 cups fresh cranberries, coarsely chopped,
   or frozen cranberries, thawed
1 tablespoon grated orange peel

CREAM CHEESE LAYER:
1 (8 ounce) package cream cheese,
   softened
⅓ cup sugar

1 egg
1 teaspoon vanilla

TOPPING:

¾ cup flour
½ cup sugar

½ cup cold butter

CAKE: Combine first four ingredients. Mix together egg, orange juice, butter, and vanilla; stir into dry ingredients until well blended. Fold in cranberries and orange peel. Pour into greased 9-inch springform pan. CREAM CHEESE LAYER: In small bowl, beat cream cheese and sugar until smooth. Add egg and vanilla; mix well. Spoon over batter. TOPPING: Combine flour and sugar. Cut in butter until mixture resembles coarse crumbs. Sprinkle over top. Place pan on baking sheet. Bake at 350 degrees for 1 hour or until golden brown. Cool on wire rack for 15 minutes before removing sides of pan.

Soft Cinnamon Rolls

ROLLS:

2 tablespoons sugar
2 packages active dry yeast
½ cup warm water
1 (3.4 ounce) package instant vanilla
  pudding
2 cups milk
½ cup butter

2 eggs, beaten
1 teaspoon salt
6 to 6½ cups flour
2 tablespoons butter, melted
½ cup brown sugar
2 teaspoons cinnamon

CARAMEL ICING:

½ cup butter
1 cup brown sugar

¼ cup milk
2 cups powdered sugar

ROLLS: Dissolve sugar and yeast in warm water. In separate bowl, mix instant pudding and milk according to package directions. Add butter, eggs, and salt into pudding mixture. Mix well and add to yeast mixture. Add flour and knead until smooth. Place in large greased mixing bowl and grease top of dough. Cover with clean cotton dish towel or plastic wrap. Let dough rise until doubled in size. Punch dough down, cover, and let rise again, about 1 hour. Punch dough down a second time and divide into 3 pieces. Roll out each piece into rectangle shape about ¼ inch thick with rolling pin. Spread with 2 tablespoons melted butter, sprinkle with ½ cup brown sugar and cinnamon. Roll up lengthwise in jelly roll fashion. Cut in 1-inch slices.* Place in greased 9-inch round baking pans. Let rise 15 minutes or until doubled in size. Bake at 350 degrees for 15 to 20 minutes or until light golden brown.
CARAMEL ICING: Melt butter in medium saucepan. Add brown sugar; bring to boil. Boil 2 minutes, stirring constantly. Add milk, stirring until mixture comes back to boil. Remove from heat and cool slightly. Stir in powdered sugar until smooth. Beat with mixer if you have trouble with it being lumpy. Spread on cooled cinnamon rolls. *Clean white thread or unflavored dental floss makes cutting dough easier.

Stuffed French Toast with Berry Sauce

This stuffed french toast will be an often-requested breakfast around your house. The creamy filling and fruity syrup make this an extraspecial treat.

FILLING:

1 (8 ounce) package cream cheese, softened
1 tablespoon sugar

1 teaspoon grated orange peel
¼ teaspoon cinnamon

FRENCH TOAST:

2 eggs, lightly beaten
¼ cup milk
1 teaspoon vanilla
8 slices day-old french bread (1 inch thick)

2 tablespoons butter
Cinnamon

SYRUP:
½ cup water
¼ cup maple syrup
2 tablespoons sugar

1 tablespoon cornstarch
1½ cups frozen blueberries

FILLING: In mixing bowl, beat cream cheese until smooth; add sugar, orange peel, and cinnamon. Mix well; set aside. FRENCH TOAST: In shallow bowl, combine eggs, milk, and vanilla. Cut each slice of bread in half, leaving a 1-inch section whole. Spread 1 to 2 tablespoons of filling inside. In large skillet, melt butter. Dip both sides of bread in egg mixture. Place in skillet; sprinkle top with additional cinnamon. Fry in hot skillet for 3 to 4 minutes on each side or until golden brown. SYRUP: Combine water, maple syrup, sugar, and cornstarch in saucepan. Bring to a boil; boil for 2 minutes or until thickened. Reduce heat; add blueberries. Simmer for 5 to 7 minutes or until berries are tender. Serve over french toast.

Blueberry Streusel Muffins

These blueberry muffins make a nice accompaniment to egg dishes for brunch or breakfast, but they also make a good snack anytime.

MUFFINS:
¼ cup butter, softened
⅓ cup sugar
1 egg
1 teaspoon vanilla
2⅓ cups flour
1 tablespoon plus 1 teaspoon baking powder

½ teaspoon salt
1 cup milk
1½ cups fresh or frozen blueberries,*
  thawed

STREUSEL TOPPING:

½ cup sugar

⅓ cup flour

½ teaspoon cinnamon

¼ cup butter, softened

MUFFINS: In mixing bowl, cream butter and sugar until light and fluffy. Add eggs and vanilla; beat well. Combine flour, baking powder, and salt; add to creamed mixture alternately with milk. Mix just until blended. Fold in blueberries. Spoon batter into greased or paper-lined muffin tins, filling two-thirds full. STREUSEL TOPPING: Combine sugar, flour, and cinnamon; cut in butter with pastry blender or fork until mixture resembles coarse crumbs. Sprinkle on top of muffin batter. Bake at 375 degrees for 25 to 30 minutes or until golden brown. Remove muffins from pan immediately. *If using frozen blueberries, rinse and drain thawed berries; pat dry with paper towels to prevent discoloration of batter.

Donut Hole Muffins

If you like donut holes, you'll like these delicious muffins. They're best eaten while they're still warm. Be warned: they're addictive.

MUFFINS:
½ cup sugar
¼ cup butter, melted
½ teaspoon nutmeg
½ cup milk
1 cup flour
1 teaspoon baking powder

TOPPING:
¼ cup butter, melted
½ cup sugar
1 teaspoon cinnamon

MUFFINS: Mix ½ cup sugar, ¼ cup butter, and nutmeg in large mixing bowl. Stir in milk. In separate bowl, combine flour and baking powder until mixed.

Stir flour mixture into creamed mixture, just until blended. Pour batter into greased 24 mini muffin cups until cups are about half full. Bake at 375 degrees for 15 to 20 minutes or until tops are lightly golden. TOPPING: While muffins are baking, melt ¼ cup butter. In separate bowl, mix together ½ cup sugar with cinnamon. Remove muffins from cups; dip each muffin in melted butter then roll in the topping mixture. Let cool.

Notes

Glorious Morning Muffins

This recipe uses applesauce in place of the normal amount of oil. The muffins are moist and chock-full of good-for-you ingredients.

2 cups flour
½ cup whole wheat flour
1¼ cups sugar
3 teaspoons cinnamon
2 teaspoons baking soda
½ teaspoon salt
3 eggs
¾ cup applesauce
½ cup vegetable oil

1 teaspoon vanilla
2 cups carrots, grated
1 medium tart apple, peeled and grated
1 (8 ounce) can crushed pineapple, drained
½ cup flaked coconut
½ cup raisins
½ cup walnuts, chopped

In large bowl, combine first six ingredients. In separate bowl, beat eggs, applesauce, oil, and vanilla. Stir in carrots, apple, pineapple, coconut, raisins, and nuts. Add wet ingredients to dry ingredients and stir until well mixed. Fill greased or paper-lined cups two-thirds full. Bake at 350 degrees for 20 to 25 minutes or until a wooden toothpick inserted comes out clean. Cool for 5 minutes before removing from pans to wire racks.

Notes

Sausage and Cheese Breakfast Strudels

Delicious flavor combination. Delicate crust.

FILLING:
2 tablespoons butter
2 tablespoons flour
1 cup milk
⅓ cup swiss or gruyère cheese, shredded
2 tablespoons parmesan cheese, grated
¼ teaspoon salt
⅛ teaspoon cayenne pepper

⅛ teaspoon nutmeg
¼ pound pork sausage
5 eggs, beaten
1½ teaspoons fresh thyme or ½ teaspoon
  dried thyme
1 tablespoon fresh parsley, chopped

PASTRY:
5 frozen phyllo pastry sheets, thawed
½ cup butter

¼ cup dry bread crumbs

TOPPING:
2 tablespoons parmesan cheese, grated
2 tablespoons fresh parsley, chopped

. . . .

FILLING: Melt 2 tablespoons butter in small saucepan. Blend in flour; cook over medium heat until smooth and bubbly, about 1 minute. Gradually add milk; cook until mixture boils and thickens, stirring constantly. Boil 1 minute. Add swiss cheese, 2 tablespoons parmesan cheese, salt, cayenne pepper, and nutmeg. Stir until cheeses are melted; set aside. In medium skillet, brown sausage and drain. Stir in eggs and thyme. Cook over medium heat until eggs are set. Stir in cheese sauce and 1 tablespoon parsley. Cool completely. PASTRY: Unroll phyllo sheets; cover with plastic wrap or towel. Brush 1 phyllo sheet with melted butter; sprinkle with bread crumbs. Fold in half lengthwise; brush with melted butter. Place ½ cup filling on bottom of short side of phyllo, leaving 1-inch edge on bottom and sides. Turn up edge; fold down sides. Roll up. Place seam side down on ungreased cookie sheet. TOPPING: In small bowl, combine parmesan cheese and parsley. Brush strudels with melted butter and sprinkle with topping. Bake at 375 degrees for 15 minutes or until crisp and light brown.

Ham and Veggie Strata

*Full of fresh veggies, this strata is a delicious way to start the day.
Vary the vegetables, meat, and cheese depending
on what you're hungry for or have on hand.*

⅓ cup vegetable oil
3 cups fresh mushrooms, sliced
3 cups zucchini, chopped
1½ cups onion, chopped
1½ cups red pepper, chopped
2 garlic cloves, minced
2 (8 ounce) packages cream cheese,
   softened

½ cup half-and-half
12 eggs
4 cups day-old bread, cubed
3 cups cheddar cheese, shredded
2 cups fully cooked ham, cubed
1 teaspoon salt
½ teaspoon pepper

In large skillet, heat oil; sauté mushrooms, zucchini, onion, red pepper, and garlic until vegetables are tender. Drain and pat dry; set aside. In large mixing bowl, beat cream cheese and half-and-half until smooth. Beat in eggs. Stir in bread, cheese, ham, salt, pepper, and vegetable mixture. Pour into two greased 7x11x2-inch baking dishes. Bake uncovered at 350 degrees for 35 to 40 minutes or until a knife inserted near the center comes out clean. Let stand for 10 minutes before serving.

Notes

....

....

....

Country Manor Tart

CRUST:
4 cups flour
1 tablespoon sugar
1 teaspoon baking powder
2 teaspoons salt
1¾ cups shortening
½ cup cold water
1 egg
1 tablespoon vinegar
1 egg white, beaten

FILLING:
8 slices bacon
1 tablespoon butter
½ cup onion, chopped
½ cup fully cooked
  smoked ham, diced
3 cups heavy cream
8 eggs, beaten
¼ teaspoon salt
¼ teaspoon pepper
¼ teaspoon nutmeg
3 tablespoons fresh basil,
  finely chopped

1 tablespoon fresh thyme,
  minced
3 ounces cream cheese,
  softened and cubed
½ cup cheddar cheese,
  shredded
½ cup Monterey Jack
  cheese, shredded
1 bunch green onions,
  chopped
⅓ cup almonds, sliced

CRUST: Mix together flour, sugar, baking powder, and salt. Cut in shortening until mixture resembles coarse crumbs. Add water, egg, and vinegar. Mix together but do not work too much. Divide pastry into two pieces, cover, and chill for 30 minutes. Form each piece into a ball and roll out crust on lightly floured surface. Carefully fit into two 10-inch tart pans. Beat egg white and brush bottom of crusts with it to help it bake. FILLING: Place bacon in large, deep skillet. Cook over medium-high heat until evenly brown. Drain, crumble, and set aside. Sauté onion in butter until translucent. Divide ham, bacon, and onion into two equal portions and sprinkle over bottom of tart shells. Whisk together cream and eggs. Add salt, pepper, nutmeg, basil, and thyme, and stir well. Pour egg mixture over bacon mixture. Sprinkle cream cheese cubes and grated cheddar and Monterey Jack cheeses over top of each filled tart. Sprinkle green onions over cheese, followed by sliced almonds. Bake at 350 degrees for 30 to 40 minutes. Let cool slightly, then cut and serve.

Pumpkin Waffles with Apple Cider Syrup

The apple cider syrup is scrumptious served on these flavorful pumpkin waffles. Top them with a dollop of whipped cream and sprinkle of cinnamon.

WAFFLES:

2½ cups flour
4 teaspoons baking powder
2½ teaspoons cinnamon
1 teaspoon allspice
1 teaspoon ginger
½ teaspoon salt

¼ cup brown sugar
1 cup canned pumpkin
2 cups milk
4 eggs, separated
¼ cup butter, melted

Apple Cider Syrup:
½ cup sugar
1 tablespoon cornstarch
1 teaspoon cinnamon

1 cup apple cider
1 tablespoon lemon juice
2 tablespoons butter

Waffles: Preheat a waffle iron according to manufacturer's instructions. Combine flour, baking powder, cinnamon, allspice, ginger, salt, and brown sugar in mixing bowl. In separate bowl, stir together pumpkin, milk, and egg yolks. Whip egg whites in clean, dry bowl until soft peaks form. Stir flour mixture and ¼ cup melted butter into pumpkin mixture, stirring just to combine. Use whisk or rubber spatula to fold one-third of the egg whites into batter, stirring gently until incorporated. Fold in remaining egg whites. Cook waffles according to manufacturer's instructions. Apple Cider Syrup: Stir together sugar, cornstarch, and cinnamon in saucepan. Stir in apple cider and lemon juice. Cook over medium heat until mixture begins to boil; boil until syrup thickens. Remove from heat and stir in 2 tablespoons of butter until melted. Serve warm.

Main and Side Dishes

Entertaining 101:

- If you're having a sit-down dinner, set the table the night before. Round up the chairs you need, and decide on a centerpiece. The next day you'll be inspired by the pretty table as you take care of last-minute preparations.

- A casual gathering means guests usually help themselves to food and drink. Turn your kitchen sink into a built-in ice chest. Plug the drain and fill with ice and an assortment of canned or bottled beverages.

- Regardless of how simply you choose to entertain, create some ambience with low lighting. Lamps, candles, and holiday lighting do this best. Just make sure you have candles safely snuffed out after your company leaves.

- If guests ask how they can help, give them a simple job to do, like filling water glasses, lighting table candles, cutting a loaf of bread, or tossing a salad. People feel more at home if you let them be involved in some way.

> When compassion for the common man
> was born on Christmas Day, with it was
> born new hope among the multitudes.
> FRANK C. LAUBACH

She shall bring forth a son, and thou shalt call his name JESUS:
for he shall save his people from their sins.
MATTHEW 1:21

Crunchy Romaine Broccoli Salad

*Crunchy is a good word to describe the texture of this delicious salad.
The dressing is light but flavorful.*

CRUNCH:
2 tablespoons butter
1 package ramen noodles
1 cup pecan halves

SALAD:
1 head romaine lettuce
1 head broccoli
4 green onions

DRESSING:
½ cup sugar
¼ cup vinegar
½ cup salad oil
1½ teaspoons soy sauce
¼ teaspoon salt
Black pepper

CRUNCH: Add butter to fry pan; fry ramen noodles and pecans until toasted. Cool. SALAD: Wash and drain lettuce and broccoli. Cut up lettuce, broccoli, and onions. DRESSING: In saucepan, heat sugar and vinegar until sugar is dissolved. Add oil, soy sauce, salt, and pepper and cool. Before serving, toss lettuce mixture with dressing, noodles, and pecans.

Notes

Winter Fruit Salad with Lemon Poppy Seed Dressing

The dressing for this salad is wonderful and simple to make. The lemon juice in the dressing helps the apple and pear pieces not to turn brown as quickly as they would otherwise.

½ cup sugar
½ cup fresh lemon juice
2 teaspoons onion, diced
1 teaspoon Dijon mustard
½ teaspoon salt
⅔ cup vegetable oil
1 tablespoon poppy seeds

1 head romaine lettuce, washed, dried, and torn into bite-sized pieces
2 cups baby greens
4 ounces swiss cheese, shredded
1 cup walnut or pecan pieces
¼ cup dried cranberries
1 apple, cored and diced
1 pear, cored and diced

In blender or food processor, combine sugar, lemon juice, onion, mustard, and salt. Process until will blended. With machine still running, add oil in a slow steady stream until mixture is thick and smooth. Add poppy seeds and process just a few seconds more to mix. In large bowl, combine romaine lettuce, baby greens, swiss cheese, nuts, dried cranberries, apple, and pear. Toss to mix; then pour dressing over salad just before serving and toss to coat.

Notes

Green Bean Mushroom Bake

A bit of a twist on the traditional green bean casserole.
The water chestnuts give it an unexpected crunch.

½ cup butter
1 pound fresh mushrooms, sliced
1 large onion, chopped
¼ cup flour
1 cup half-and-half
1 (16 ounce) jar processed cheese sauce
2 teaspoons soy sauce

½ teaspoon pepper
⅛ teaspoon hot pepper sauce
1 (8 ounce) can sliced water chestnuts, drained
2 (16 ounce) packages frozen french-style green beans, thawed and drained
Slivered almonds

In skillet, heat butter; sauté mushrooms and onion in butter. Stir in flour until blended. Gradually stir in half-and-half. Bring to a boil. Cook and stir for 2 minutes, stirring constantly. Stir in cheese sauce, soy sauce, pepper, and hot sauce until cheese is melted. Remove from heat; stir in water chestnuts. Place beans in greased 3-quart casserole baking dish. Pour cheese mixture over top. Sprinkle with almonds. Bake uncovered at 375 degrees for 25 to 30 minutes or until bubbly.

Notes

Loaded Mashed Potato Casserole

*This is a delicious way to use leftover mashed potatoes.
If you don't have leftovers, it's worth making a fresh
batch for this flavorful comfort food casserole.*

2 tablespoons butter
1 onion, chopped
4 ounces cream cheese, softened
4 cups prepared mashed potatoes
1 egg, beaten
1 tablespoon flour

¼ teaspoon salt
⅛ teaspoon pepper
1 cup cheddar cheese, shredded
6 pieces bacon, fried and crumbled
½ can (6 ounces) french fried onions
Chives

In medium skillet, melt butter and fry onions until tender. In large bowl, beat cream cheese until smooth; add mashed potatoes, onion, egg, flour, salt, and pepper. Beat 2 to 3 minutes, until well mixed. Pour into greased 3-quart casserole dish. Sprinkle with cheese and crumbled bacon. Spread fried onions evenly over top. Bake uncovered at 300 degrees for 45 minutes. If desired, garnish with chives.

Notes

Ravioli with Sage Cream Sauce

Salt
2 (8 to 9 ounce) packages of refrigerated
  or frozen ravioli, thawed
3 tablespoons butter
½ cup pecans, chopped
⅔ cup shallots, finely chopped

3 tablespoons fresh sage, finely chopped
1½ cups dry white wine
1⅓ cups whipping cream
Black pepper
Chopped pecans
Parmesan cheese shavings

Cook ravioli in large pot of salted, boiling water until just tender but still firm to bite, about 8 minutes. Drain well. Melt butter in heavy medium skillet over medium heat. Add pecans and stir until slightly darker and fragrant, about 3 minutes. Using slotted spoon, transfer pecans to small bowl. Add shallots and sage to same skillet. Sauté until fragrant, about 30 seconds. Add wine and cream; increase heat and boil until sauce reduces to generous 1½ cups, about 5 to 7 minutes. Add ravioli to sauce; toss. Season with salt and pepper. Sprinkle with pecans and cheese shavings. Serve immediately.

Notes

Sweet Potato Orange Cups

Sugar-Coated Pecans:
1 egg white
½ tablespoon water
½ cup sugar
¼ teaspoon salt
½ teaspoon cinnamon
½ pound pecan halves

Orange Cups:
7 medium oranges

Filling:
3 cups sweet potatoes, cooked and
    mashed
¾ cup sugar
¼ cup orange juice
2 eggs, slightly beaten
1 teaspoon vanilla
¼ cup butter, melted
1 tablespoon grated orange peel
Mint leaves

- -

Sugar-Coated Pecans: Whip egg white and water in small bowl until frothy.

In separate bowl, mix together sugar, salt, and cinnamon. Add pecan halves to egg whites; stir until nuts are evenly coated. Remove nuts and toss them in sugar mixture until coated. Spread nuts on greased baking sheet. Bake at 250 degrees for 1 hour, stirring every 15 minutes. Set aside and let cool. ORANGE CUPS: Prepare oranges by cutting in half and squeezing out juice. Reserve ¼ cup of juice; scoop insides out of orange halves. FILLING: In large bowl, combine sweet potatoes, sugar, orange juice, eggs, vanilla, butter, and orange peel. Spoon mixture into hollowed-out orange halves. Place orange halves in 9x13-inch baking dish and add ¼ inch water. Bake at 350 degrees for 30 minutes. Remove from oven and top each orange half with 3 sugar-coated pecan halves and a leaf of mint in the middle.

Spinach Penne Toss

*Wonderful as a side dish, or add a marinated
grilled chicken breast and make it a meal.*

2 cups uncooked penne pasta
1 tablespoon plus ¼ cup olive oil, divided
1 medium sweet red pepper, julienned
1 medium onion, sliced
1 package (6 ounces) fresh baby spinach
¾ cup bacon, fried and crumbled

½ cup feta cheese, crumbled
½ cup oil-packed sun-dried
   tomatoes, chopped
2 tablespoons cider vinegar
¼ teaspoon pepper
⅛ teaspoon salt

Cook pasta according to package directions. Meanwhile, in large skillet, heat
1 tablespoon oil; sauté red pepper and onion for 3 to 4 minutes or until

tender. Drain pasta and place in serving bowl. Add red pepper mixture,
spinach, bacon, feta cheese, and tomatoes. In small bowl, whisk vinegar,
pepper, salt, and remaining oil. Drizzle over pasta mixture; toss to coat.

Notes

Cider-Glazed Brussels Sprouts

Even people that don't like brussels sprouts like these.
The dressing and bacon have a sweet-salty combination.

4 slices bacon, chopped
1 tablespoon butter
1 small red onion, thinly sliced
2 pounds brussels sprouts, trimmed
  and halved
¾ cup apple cider

¼ cup sugar
½ teaspoon salt
¼ teaspoon nutmeg
¼ teaspoon freshly ground black pepper
¼ cup almonds, sliced and toasted

Fry bacon in large skillet until crisp. Remove bacon from skillet with slotted spoon; drain on paper towels. Discard all but 1 tablespoon drippings from skillet. Add butter, onions, and brussels sprouts to drippings in skillet; cook on medium-high heat 1 to 2 minutes or until brussels sprouts are lightly browned, stirring occasionally. Mix next five ingredients; pour over sprouts. Cook 5 minutes or until liquid is evaporated and sprouts are evenly glazed, stirring occasionally. Stir in bacon. Spoon sprouts into bowl. Top with nuts.

Notes

Chicken and Bowtie Pasta in Cream Sauce

Bowtie pasta is a family favorite.
Paired with salad and crusty bread, you can't go wrong.

12 ounces farfalle (bowtie) pasta
2 tablespoons olive oil
1½ pounds skinless boneless chicken
  breasts, cubed
2½ cups heavy whipping cream, divided
1 cube chicken bouillon, crumbled
1 cup Asiago cheese, grated

½ tablespoon cornstarch
2 tablespoons water
2 tablespoons butter
½ cup prosciutto, chopped
1 tablespoon fresh garlic, chopped
1 cup baby portobello mushrooms, sliced
½ tablespoon parsley flakes

Cook pasta according to directions on box. Drain and set aside. Heat olive oil in skillet over medium heat. Cook chicken cubes until no longer pink in center and juices run clear. Set aside. In medium saucepan, bring 2 cups cream to a simmer, stirring often. Whisk in bouillon cube and cheese until bouillon has dissolved and cheese is well blended. Dissolve cornstarch in water, and whisk into cream mixture. Cook and stir 2 minutes more; then remove from heat and set aside. Melt butter in skillet used to fry chicken over medium heat. Stir in prosciutto, garlic, and mushrooms; sauté until mushrooms are tender; about 3 minutes. Add chicken, reduce heat, and continue cooking until chicken is heated through. Return sauce to heat and add remaining ½ cup cream and parsley flakes. Heat through. To serve, place pasta in large serving bowl. Add chicken and mushroom mixture and pour cream sauce over top. Toss well and serve.

Beef Tenderloin with Shallots in Wine Sauce

When a special occasion calls for something extraordinary, this is the recipe to pull. Serve with garlic mashed potatoes and a vegetable. Sure to impress your guests.

¾ pound shallots, halved lengthwise and peeled
1½ tablespoons olive oil
Salt and pepper to taste
3 cups beef broth
¾ cup port wine
1½ teaspoons tomato paste

2 pounds beef tenderloin, trimmed
1 teaspoon dried thyme
3 slices bacon, diced
2 pounds baby portobello mushrooms, cleaned and sliced
3 tablespoons butter, divided
1 tablespoon flour

In 9-inch pie pan, toss shallots with oil to coat. Season with salt and pepper.

Roast until shallots are deep brown and very tender, stirring occasionally, about 30 minutes. In large saucepan, combine beef broth and port wine. Bring to boil. Cook over high heat until volume is reduced by half, about 30 minutes. Whisk in tomato paste. Set aside. Pat beef dry; sprinkle with thyme, salt, and pepper. In large roasting pan, over medium heat, fry bacon. Add mushrooms and sauté until bacon is crisp and mushrooms are tender. Using a slotted spoon, transfer bacon and mushrooms to paper towel to drain. When drained, place shallots, bacon, and broth mixture in blender; puree. Place beef into pan to brown on all sides over medium heat, about 7 minutes. Put pan in preheated oven at 375 degrees for 25 minutes or until a meat thermometer registers 125 degrees for medium rare, longer for how you want your meat done. Transfer meat to platter. Tent loosely with foil. Spoon fat off the top of pan drippings in roasting pan. Place pan over high heat on stove top. Add broth and shallot mixture and bring to boil; stir to deglaze pan. Transfer to medium saucepan; simmer. Mix 1½ tablespoons butter and flour in small bowl to form smooth paste; whisk into broth mixture and simmer until sauce thickens. Whisk in remaining butter. Cut beef into ½-inch slices. Spoon sauce over beef. Garnish.

Chicken Marsala

4 chicken breasts
3 tablespoons flour
1¼ teaspoons salt
1 teaspoon ground black pepper
½ teaspoon dried oregano
½ teaspoon dried thyme
½ teaspoon dried parsley
¼ teaspoon marjoram
¼ teaspoon garlic powder
2 tablespoons olive oil

⅓ cup butter
1 slice prosciutto, diced
1 cup of fresh mushrooms, wiped clean
   and sliced
2 teaspoons minced shallots
2 teaspoons minced garlic
1 cup marsala cooking wine
¼ cup chicken stock
2 teaspoons cornstarch
2 tablespoons heavy cream

Pound chicken pieces to ¼-inch thickness (place between 2 sheets wax paper before pounding). Combine flour, salt, pepper, oregano, thyme, parsley, marjoram, and garlic powder. Use your thumb and fingers to crush spices to make a fine blend. Dredge chicken pieces in flour mixture. Heat 2 tablespoons olive oil in large skillet over medium-high heat. Fry chicken 8 to 10 minutes or until juices run clear. Remove from pan. Keep warm in oven. In same skillet, melt butter over low heat. When melted, turn heat up to medium high; add prosciutto and mushrooms. Sauté 2 to 3 minutes; add shallots and garlic and continue sautéing for an additional 30 seconds. Stir in marsala wine; simmer over medium heat for 5 minutes. In saucepan, heat chicken stock; dissolve cornstarch in stock. Stir stock into skillet and simmer for an additional 5 minutes. Add cream to sauce and simmer 3 to 4 minutes or until thickened. Spoon one-quarter sauce over each serving of chicken and serve.

Honey Herb-Glazed Chicken

Mildly sweet glaze turns crispy as it bakes.

1 (16 pound) whole turkey, neck and
  giblets removed
¼ cup olive oil
1 teaspoon salt
¼ teaspoon pepper
1 teaspoon ground thyme
1 cup honey

½ cup butter, melted
2 teaspoons sage
1 tablespoon fresh parsley, minced
1 teaspoon basil
1 teaspoon salt
1 teaspoon pepper

Rinse turkey; pat thoroughly with dry paper towels. Brush turkey with olive oil, inside and out. Mix 1 teaspoon salt, ¼ teaspoon pepper, and thyme;

sprinkle mixture on turkey. Place turkey on rack set in roasting pan, and roast in 325-degree oven for 2 hours. In small bowl, stir together honey, melted butter, sage, parsley, basil, 1 teaspoon salt, and 1 teaspoon pepper until mixture is smooth and well blended. Brush turkey with honey glaze and return to oven. Roast turkey until no longer pink and juices run clear, about 2 more hours. An instant-read thermometer inserted into thickest part of thigh, near the bone, should read 180 degrees. Continue to brush turkey with glaze frequently as it roasts. Remove turkey from oven, cover with a double sheet of aluminum foil, and allow to rest in a warm area 10 to 15 minutes before slicing.

Chicken Divan

This is a festive-looking dish, with the green of the broccoli and red of the pimento. Serve it over rice.

1½ pounds chicken, cooked and shredded
2 (10 ounce) packages broccoli, cooked and drained
¼ cup butter
2 tablespoons onion, minced
¼ cup flour
¼ teaspoon salt
⅛ teaspoon pepper

1¼ cups chicken broth
1 cup half-and-half
2 egg yolks
1 tablespoon parmesan cheese
¾ cup swiss cheese, grated and divided
Paprika
1 (4 ounce) jar pimento, drained

Arrange chicken in bottom of greased 9x13-inch baking dish; cover with broccoli. Melt butter in saucepan; add onion and sauté until tender. Add flour, salt, and pepper. Cook 1 minute, stirring constantly. Gradually add chicken broth and half-and-half, stirring to keep smooth. Cook until thick. Stir a little sauce in yolks, return yolk mixture to pan; mix will. Stir in parmesan cheese and ½ cup swiss cheese; heat until cheese melts. Pour sauce over broccoli. Sprinkle with paprika and remaining swiss cheese. Bake at 350 degrees for 20 to 30 minutes. Garnish with pimento, if desired.

Notes

....

....

Seafood Lasagna

If you want to impress your guests,
this seafood lasagna is a wonderful choice.

2 tablespoons butter
1 green onion, finely chopped
½ cup chicken broth
1 (8 ounce) bottle clam juice
1 pound bay scallops
1 pound uncooked small shrimp, peeled
    and deveined
1 (8 ounce) package imitation crabmeat,
    chopped

¼ teaspoon white pepper, divided
½ cup butter
½ cup flour
1½ cups milk
½ teaspoon salt
1 cup heavy whipping cream
½ cup shredded parmesan cheese, divided
12 lasagna noodles, cooked and drained

In large skillet, melt butter; sauté onion until tender. Stir in broth and clam juice; bring to boil. Add scallops, shrimp, crabmeat, and ⅛ teaspoon pepper; return to boil. Reduce heat; simmer uncovered for 25 minutes or until shrimp turn pink and scallops are firm and opaque, stirring gently. Drain, reserving cooking liquid; set seafood mixture aside. In large saucepan, melt ½ cup butter; stir in flour until smooth. Combine milk and reserved cooking liquid; gradually add to saucepan. Add salt and remaining pepper. Bring to boil; cook and stir for 2 minutes or until thickened. Remove from heat; stir in whipping cream and ¼ cup cheese. Stir ¾ cup white sauce into seafood mixture. Spread ½ cup white sauce in greased 9x13-inch baking dish. Top with 4 noodles; spread with half of seafood mixture and 1¼ cups sauce. Repeat layers. Top with remaining noodles, sauce, and cheese. Bake uncovered at 350 degrees for 35 to 40 minutes or until golden brown. Let stand 15 minutes before cutting.

Lasagna Roll-Ups

Individual lasagna roll-ups are an easy way to avoid the messy appearance of traditional lasagna. They look pretty and taste delicious.

¼ pound ground beef
¼ pound Italian sausage
2 tablespoons onion, chopped
1 garlic clove, minced
1 (16 ounce) can crushed tomatoes
½ teaspoon salt
½ teaspoon dried oregano
Dash cayenne pepper

1¼ cups small curd cottage cheese,
   drained or ricotta cheese
¼ cup parmesan cheese, grated
1 egg, lightly beaten
1 tablespoon fresh parsley, minced
¼ teaspoon onion powder
6 lasagna noodles, cooked and drained
½ cup mozzarella cheese, shredded

In medium skillet, cook beef, sausage, onion, and garlic until meat is no longer pink; drain. Add tomatoes, salt, oregano, and cayenne pepper; simmer for 10 minutes. Spoon half of meat sauce into greased 9-inch square baking dish. Combine cottage or ricotta cheese, parmesan cheese, egg, parsley, and onion powder; spread ¼ cup on each noodle. Carefully roll up and place seam side down over meat sauce. Top with remaining meat sauce. Sprinkle with mozzarella cheese. Cover and bake at 375 degrees for 30 to 35 minutes or until heated through. Let stand 10 minutes before serving.

Notes

Desserts

Entertaining 101:

- A meringue (such as what appears on the cover of this book) is made up of egg whites and sugar.

- Use a clean, dry bowl (glass, ceramic, stainless steel, or copper). Plastic bowls may appear clean but may still have trace amounts of oil, so do not use them.

- Cold eggs separate easily, but eggs whip to a higher volume when at room temperature. For best results, separate the cold eggs, and then set them aside for 10 or 15 minutes before whipping.

- Some of your guests will bring a hostess gift. Accept it graciously and with thanks, even if the gift is something you cannot use. You can always give it away later to someone who will appreciate it.

- A good time to move your guests into another room for conversation and a change of position is before that second round of coffee. Encourage them to bring along their coffee or tea, and freshen drinks once everyone is settled.

- If the meal you are planning is heavy, make dessert very light, and vice versa.

When they were come into the house, they saw the young child with Mary his mother, and fell down, and worshipped him.
MATTHEW 2:11

Cranberry Pistachio Christmas Biscotti

Place a few in a pretty cellophane bag and tie with ribbon.
Put the bag in a festive mug and you have an inexpensive gift.

¼ cup light olive oil
¾ cup sugar
2 teaspoons vanilla
½ teaspoon almond extract
2 eggs
1¾ cups flour

¼ teaspoon salt
1 teaspoon baking powder
1 cup dried cranberries, coarsely chopped
1 cup pistachio nuts, coarsely chopped
White chocolate chips

In large bowl, mix together oil and sugar until well blended. Mix in vanilla and almond extract; beat in eggs. Combine flour, salt, and baking powder;

gradually stir into egg mixture. Mix in cranberries and nuts by hand. Divide dough in half. Form two logs (12x2 inches) on a cookie sheet lined with parchment paper. Dough may be sticky; wet hands with cool water to handle dough more easily. Bake at 300 degrees for 35 minutes or until logs are light brown. Remove from oven; set aside to cool for 10 minutes. Reduce oven heat to 275 degrees. Cut logs on diagonal into ¾-inch slices. Lay on sides on parchment-covered cookie sheet. Bake for approximately 8 to 10 minutes or until dry; cool. Melt white chocolate chips in microwave, stirring frequently until chocolate is melted. Dip end of biscotti in melted chocolate.

Peanut Butter Brownie Pie

If you like peanut butter and chocolate, this is the pie for you. It is very rich, so you may want cut it in small pieces. A much-requested recipe.

1 unbaked 9-inch pie shell
1 (15.5 ounce) package chocolate chunk
   brownie mix
¼ cup peanut butter chips
⅓ cup vegetable oil
3 tablespoons water
1 egg
1 (8 ounce) package cream cheese,
   softened

½ cup creamy peanut butter
1 cup powdered sugar
½ cup heavy whipping cream
2 tablespoons peanuts, chopped
2 tablespoons mini semisweet
   chocolate chips

In medium bowl, stir brownie mix, peanut butter chips, oil, water, and egg 50 strokes with spoon. Pour batter into pie shell. Bake at 350 degrees for 30 to 40 minutes, covering edge of crust with strips of foil after 15 to 20 minutes, until crust is golden brown and center of pie is set. Cool slightly, about 20 minutes. Refrigerate 1 hour or until completely cooled. In medium bowl, beat cream cheese, peanut butter, and powdered sugar with electric mixer on medium speed until smooth. Add whipping cream and beat until fluffy. Spread mixture over brownie. Sprinkle with peanuts and chocolate chips.

Notes

Maple Pumpkin Cheesecake

CRUST:
3⁄4 cup pecans, finely chopped
32 gingersnap cookies, coarsely chopped

3 tablespoons brown sugar
6 tablespoons butter, melted

FILLING:
3 (8 ounce) packages cream cheese,
   softened
1 cup brown sugar, packed
1½ cups canned pumpkin
½ cup heavy whipping cream
¼ cup maple syrup

3 teaspoons vanilla
1 teaspoon cinnamon
½ teaspoon ginger
¼ teaspoon cloves
4 eggs, lightly beaten

Topping:

½ cup heavy whipping cream

2 tablespoons powdered sugar

1 teaspoon vanilla

12 pieces of pecan brittle, purchased

CRUST: Mix pecans, gingersnaps, brown sugar, and butter. Press in bottom and 2 inches up sides of greased 9-inch springform pan; set aside. FILLING: In large bowl, beat cream cheese until smooth; add brown sugar until mixed. Beat in pumpkin, whipping cream, maple syrup, vanilla, and spices. Add eggs, one at a time; mix on low speed just until combined. Pour into crust. Fill shallow baking dish with 1 inch of water and place on lower rack. This helps keep cheesecake from cracking. Bake at 325 degrees for 70 to 80 minutes or until center is just set and top appears dull. Turn oven off and open oven door. Allow cheesecake to cool in oven for 1 hour. Carefully run knife around edge of pan to loosen. Refrigerate at least 6 hours or overnight. TOPPING: When ready to serve, whip heavy whipping cream until it forms stiff peaks. Stir in powdered sugar and vanilla. Cut cheesecake; spoon a dollop of whipped cream on each slice and a piece of pecan brittle inserted sideways in middle of whipped cream.

Layered Mocha Cheesecake

Rich and creamy! A coffee lover's dream.

CRUST:
1½ cups cream-filled chocolate
  sandwich cookie crumbs
¼ cup butter, melted

GLAZE:
½ cup (3 ounces) semisweet chocolate
  chips
3 tablespoons butter
Chocolate-covered coffee beans,
  optional

FILLING:
2½ tablespoons instant coffee granules
1 tablespoon boiling water
¼ teaspoon cinnamon
4 (8 ounce) packages cream cheese
1½ cups sugar
¼ cup flour
2 teaspoons vanilla
4 eggs, lightly beaten
2 cups (12 ounces) semisweet chocolate
  chips, melted and cooled

CRUST: Combine cookie crumbs and butter; press onto the bottom of a greased 9-inch springform pan. FILLING: In small bowl, combine coffee granules, water, and cinnamon; set aside. In large bowl, beat softened cream cheese until smooth. Add sugar, flour, and vanilla and mix well. Add eggs, one at a time; mix on low speed just until blended. Divide batter in half. Stir melted chocolate into one portion; pour over crust. Stir coffee mixture into the remaining batter; spoon over chocolate layer. Fill shallow baking dish with 1 inch of water and place on lower rack of oven. This helps keep cheesecake from cracking. Bake at 325 degrees for 55 to 60 minutes or until center is just set and top appears dull. Turn off oven and open oven door. Cool in oven for 1 hour. Remove from oven and carefully run knife around edge of pan. Refrigerate overnight. GLAZE: In microwave-safe bowl, melt chocolate and butter. Stir until smooth. Spread over cheesecake. Garnish edge with coffee beans if desired.

Cranberry Bread Pudding with Orange Sauce

A wonderfully comforting dessert, full of the flavors of the season.

BREAD PUDDING:
1 loaf day-old french bread, cubed
1½ cups fresh or thawed frozen cranberries
1 tablespoon grated orange peel
¼ cup butter, melted

6 eggs
4 cups half-and-half
13 tablespoons sugar, divided
1 teaspoon vanilla

ORANGE CUSTARD SAUCE:
3 egg yolks
¼ cup sugar
1 cup whipping cream

1 orange peel strip (¼ inch)
½ teaspoon orange extract

BREAD PUDDING: In greased 9x13-inch baking dish, layer half of the bread cubes, cranberries, and orange peel. Repeat layers. Drizzle with butter. In large mixing bowl, beat eggs, half-and-half, ¾ cup sugar, and vanilla; pour over bread mixture. Let stand for 15 to 30 minutes. Sprinkle with remaining sugar. Bake uncovered at 375 degrees for 60 to 70 minutes or until knife inserted near the center comes out clean. ORANGE CUSTARD SAUCE: In heavy saucepan, beat egg yolks and sugar. Stir in cream and orange peel. Cook and stir over low heat for 20 to 25 minutes or until mixture reaches 160 degrees and coats the back of a metal spoon. Remove from heat; discard orange peel. Stir in extract. Cover and refrigerate until chilled. Serve over bread pudding.

Gingerbread Pumpkin Trifle

GINGERBREAD:
½ cup shortening
⅓ cup sugar
1 cup molasses
1 egg
2⅓ cups flour

1 teaspoon baking soda
1 teaspoon ginger
1 teaspoon cinnamon
¾ teaspoon salt
¾ cup hot water

FILLING:
2 cups cold milk
1 (3.4 ounce) package instant vanilla
   pudding
1 (15 ounce) can pumpkin

½ cup brown sugar
1 teaspoon vanilla
½ teaspoon cinnamon

TOPPING:
2 cups heavy whipping cream   1 teaspoon vanilla or rum extract
⅓ cup powdered sugar

GINGERBREAD: In large bowl, cream shortening and sugar until light and fluffy. Beat in molasses and egg. Combine flour, baking soda, ginger, cinnamon, and salt; add to creamed mixture alternately with water, beating well after each addition. Pour into greased 9x13-inch baking pan. Bake at 350 degrees for 25 to 30 minutes or until toothpick inserted near the center comes out clean. Cool on wire rack. Cut gingerbread into ½-inch cubes; set aside. FILLING: In large bowl, whisk milk and pudding; mix for 2 minutes. Let stand 2 minutes or until soft-set. Combine pumpkin, brown sugar, vanilla, and cinnamon; stir into pudding. TOPPING: In another bowl, beat cream until it begins to thicken. Add sugar and extract; beat until stiff peaks form. Set aside ¼ cup gingerbread cubes. In 4-quart trifle bowl or glass serving bowl, layer a third of the remaining gingerbread cubes; top with a third of the pumpkin filling mixture and whipped cream topping. Repeat layers twice. Crumble reserved gingerbread; sprinkle over top. Cover and refrigerate for at least 1 hour before serving.

Cherry Pretzel Dessert

"Sweet and salty" is a good way to describe this pretty dessert. It has a yummy pretzel crust topped with a sweet cherry filling. Cherry filling can be switched to another red fruit topping such as raspberry or strawberry.

CRUST:
2 cups pretzels, crushed
¼ cup sugar
½ cup butter, melted

TOPPING:
1 (21 ounce) can cherry pie filling

FILLING:
1 (12 ounce) can sweetened condensed milk
½ cup water
1 (3.4 ounce) package instant vanilla pudding
1 (4 ounce) container frozen whipped topping, thawed

CRUST: In large bowl, combine all crust ingredients; mix well. Press in bottom of ungreased 9x13-inch pan. Bake at 350 degrees for 8 minutes. Cool 10 minutes. FILLING: In same large bowl, combine condensed milk and water; blend well. Add pudding mix; beat 2 minutes with electric mixer at medium speed. Refrigerate 5 minutes. Fold whipped topping into thickened pudding mixture. Spread pudding over cooled baked crust. Refrigerate about 1 hour or until filling is firm. TOPPING: Spoon cherry pie filling over pudding filling. Cover; refrigerate at least 1 hour or until serving time. If desired, garnish each serving with additional whipped topping and a tree-shaped pretzel dipped in chocolate.

Cream Puffs

For a lighter dessert, turn to these. You can be very creative with cream puffs.
Use different flavored fillings depending on the main course;
or fill the shells with tuna or chicken salad and use them for an appetizer.

PUDDING:
2½ cups milk
¾ cup sugar
4 tablespoons cornstarch
½ teaspoon salt
½ cup milk
3 egg yolks, slightly beaten
1 teaspoon vanilla
1 tablespoon butter

PUFFS:
1 cup water
½ cup butter
1 cup flour
4 eggs

PUDDING: Heat 2½ cups milk and sugar to boiling point. In bowl, mix cornstarch, salt, ½ cup milk, and eggs yolks with mixer and add to hot milk. Cook over medium heat until thickened, stirring constantly. Remove from heat and add vanilla and butter. Cool completely. PUFFS: In medium saucepan, heat water and butter to a rolling boil. Add flour, stirring vigorously over low heat about 1 minute or until mixture forms a ball. Remove from heat. Beat in eggs all at one time; continue beating until smooth. Use melon scooper or tablespoon to drop dough about 3 inches apart on parchment paper–covered baking sheets. Bake at 425 degrees for 20 to 25 minutes or until puffed and golden. Remove from oven and poke hole in side of each puff with toothpick to allow steam to escape. Cool. Cut in half and fill middle with cooled vanilla pudding. Drizzle with chocolate ice cream topping if desired.

Date Pudding

This holiday dessert looks very pretty layered in a glass trifle bowl.

CAKE:
1 cup dates, chopped
1 cup boiling water
1 teaspoon baking soda
1 egg
1 cup brown sugar
1 tablespoon butter
1 cup flour
1 teaspoon vanilla
½ cup walnuts, chopped

BUTTERSCOTCH SAUCE:
2 tablespoons butter
¾ cup brown sugar
1 cup water
2 tablespoons clear jell
1 egg yolk, slightly beaten
2 cups milk
Pinch of salt

WHIPPED CREAM:
2 cups heavy whipping cream   1 teaspoon vanilla
⅓ cup powdered sugar

....

CAKE: Mix together dates, boiling water, and baking soda; set aside. In
bowl, combine egg, brown sugar, butter, flour, vanilla, and walnuts. Add
date mixture and mix. Pour into shallow cake pan and bake at 350 degrees
for 15 to 20 minutes or until a toothpick inserted near center comes out
clean. Cool and cut into small squares. BUTTERSCOTCH SAUCE: To make
butterscotch sauce, melt butter and brown sugar in saucepan. Add water; let
cook until ingredients are dissolved. Mix clear jell, egg yolk, milk, and salt.
Stir into brown sugar mixture; cook until thickened, stirring constantly. Cool.
WHIPPED CREAM: Beat whipping cream until stiff peaks form. Add sugar
and vanilla; mix. In trifle or glass bowl, layer cake, butterscotch sauce, and
whipped cream until bowl is full, ending with whipped cream. Sprinkle with
additional chopped walnuts. You can also add layers of bananas if desired.
Refrigerate until ready to serve.

Homemade Apple Dumplings

SAUCE:
2 cups sugar
2 cups water
½ teaspoon cinnamon
¼ cup butter

CRUST:
2 cups flour
2½ teaspoons baking powder
½ teaspoon salt
⅔ cup shortening
½ cup milk

FILLING: (per apple)
Dab butter
1 teaspoon brown sugar
Dash cinnamon

3 medium apples, peeled, cored, and halved

Sauce: Mix sauce ingredients in saucepan; simmer for 5 minutes and set aside. Prepare apples. Crust: Mix flour, baking powder, and salt, then cut in shortening until it forms small beads. Add milk. Roll and cut into 5-inch squares. Filling: Place an apple on each square and fill center of apple with filling ingredients. Wrap dough over apple, pinch to seal. Arrange dumplings in greased 9x13-inch baking dish. Pour sauce over each dumpling. Bake at 375 degrees for 35 to 40 minutes. Baste several times while baking.

Notes

Chocolate-Almond Ice Cream Roll

CAKE:

⅓ cup flour
¼ cup unsweetened cocoa powder
1 teaspoon baking powder
¼ teaspoon salt
4 large egg yolks (save whites)
½ teaspoon vanilla extract

⅓ cup sugar
4 large egg whites
½ cup sugar
Sifted powdered sugar
1 quart butter-almond or chocolate-almond ice cream, softened

SAUCE:

1 (12 ounce) package frozen loose-pack red raspberries, thawed
¾ cup sugar

1 teaspoon lemon juice
Melted white chocolate (optional)
Fresh raspberries (optional)

CAKE: In bowl, stir together dry ingredients. Set aside. In small mixing bowl, beat egg yolks and vanilla on high speed about 5 minutes or until lemon colored. Gradually add ⅓ cup sugar, beating on medium speed 5 minutes or until sugar is almost dissolved. In large mixing bowl, beat egg whites on medium speed until soft peaks form (tips curl). Gradually add ½ cup sugar, beating on high speed until stiff peaks form (tips stand straight). Fold egg yolk mixture into beaten egg whites. Sprinkle flour mixture over egg mixture; fold in gently just until combined. Spread batter evenly in greased 10x15x1-inch baking pan. Bake at 375 degrees for 12 to 15 minutes or until top springs back when lightly touched. Immediately loosen edges of cake from pan; turn out onto towel sprinkled with powdered sugar. Roll up towel and cake, starting from short side. Cool on wire rack. Unroll cake. Spread softened ice cream on cake to within 1 inch of edges. Roll up cake without towel. Wrap in foil; freeze 4 hours or up to one week. SAUCE: In blender or food processor, blend thawed raspberries on high speed until smooth. Press through strainer to remove seeds. In small saucepan, stir together raspberry puree, ¾ cup sugar, and lemon juice. Bring mixture to boil over medium-low heat. Boil 3 minutes, stirring constantly. To serve, place slices on dessert plates. Spoon sauce next to each slice. If desired, decorate sauce using melted white chocolate and garnish with raspberries.

Gingerbread Topped with Amber Cream

GINGERBREAD:
½ cup shortening
½ cup sugar
2 eggs
1 cup molasses
1 cup water
2⅓ cups flour

1 teaspoon baking powder
1 teaspoon baking soda
1 teaspoon salt
1 teaspoon cinnamon
1 teaspoon ginger
½ teaspoon cloves

AMBER CREAM:
1 cup whipping cream
⅓ cup brown sugar

1 teaspoon vanilla
Nutmeg

GINGERBREAD: In mixing bowl, cream shortening and sugar until fluffy. Add eggs, one at a time, beating well after each addition. Mix molasses and water. Combine dry ingredients; add to creamed mixture alternately with molasses mixture; beat just until blended. Pour into greased 9x13-inch baking pan. Bake at 350 degrees for 30 to 35 minutes or until toothpick inserted near the center comes out clean. AMBER CREAM: In small mixing bowl, combine cream, brown sugar and vanilla; chill for at least 1 hour. Whip until stiff peaks form. Top each piece of gingerbread with a spoonful of whipped cream and sprinkle with a little nutmeg.

Macadamia Nut Lemon Bars

*Melt-in-your-mouth lemon flavor makes these
pretty bars a favorite wherever they are served.*

BARS:
1 cup flour
¼ cup powdered sugar

½ cup butter, melted
¼ cup macadamia nuts, chopped

FILLING:
1 cup sugar
2 tablespoons flour
½ teaspoon baking powder
¼ teaspoon salt
2 eggs

2 tablespoons lemon juice
2 teaspoons grated lemon peel
2 tablespoons macadamia nuts, chopped
Powdered sugar

Bars: In bowl, combine flour, powdered sugar, and butter; stir in ¼ cup nuts. Press onto bottom and ½ inch up sides of greased 8-inch square baking pan. Bake at 350 degrees for 12 to 15 minutes or until lightly browned. Filling: In small mixing bowl, combine sugar, flour, baking powder, and salt. Beat in eggs, lemon juice, and lemon peel until light and fluffy. Pour over hot crust. Sprinkle with nuts. Bake at 350 degrees for 10 to 15 minutes or until lightly browned. Cool completely. Cut into bars. Sprinkle with powdered sugar.

Notes

Sour Cream Raisin Bars

CRUMBS:
1¾ cups oatmeal
1¾ cups flour
1 cup brown sugar
1 cup butter, softened
1 teaspoon soda
1 teaspoon baking powder
Pinch salt

FILLING:
4 eggs, beaten
1 cup sugar
1 tablespoon cornstarch
2 cups sour cream
1½ cups raisins
1 teaspoon vanilla

CRUMBS: Combine all crumb ingredients. Pat ⅔ cup crumbs in greased 9x13-inch baking dish. Bake at 350 degrees for 15 minutes. Cool. FILLING: In medium saucepan, mix filling ingredients together. Bring to boil, stirring constantly. Pour over crumb crust. Cover with remaining crumbs and bake for another 15 to 20 minutes. Cool and cut into bars.

Notes

Pumpkin Roll

CAKE:
3 eggs
1 cup sugar
¾ cup canned pumpkin
1 teaspoon lemon juice
¾ cup flour
2 teaspoons cinnamon
1 teaspoon baking powder
1 teaspoon ginger
1 teaspoon salt
½ teaspoon nutmeg
Powdered sugar

CREAM CHEESE FILLING:
1 (8 ounce) package cream cheese, softened
1 cup powdered sugar
¼ cup butter, softened
½ teaspoon vanilla
Additional powdered sugar

CAKE: In large bowl, beat eggs on high for 5 minutes. Gradually beat in sugar until thick and lemon colored. Add pumpkin and lemon juice. In separate bowl, combine flour, cinnamon, baking powder, ginger, salt, and nutmeg; fold into pumpkin mixture. Grease 10x15x1-inch baking pan and line with waxed paper. Grease and flour paper. Spread batter into pan. Bake at 375 degrees for 15 minutes or until cake springs back when lightly touched. Immediately turn out onto a linen towel dusted with powdered sugar. Peel off paper and roll cake up in towel, starting with a short end. Cool. CREAM CHEESE FILLING: In another bowl, beat cream cheese until smooth; add sugar, butter, and vanilla. Beat until fluffy. Carefully unroll cake. Spread filling over cake to within 1 inch of edges. Roll up again. Cover and chill until serving. Dust with powdered sugar.

Appetizers

Entertaining 101:

- Always use unscented candles when you entertain. The perfumed types can be overpowering and can even distaste the food you serve. The wonderful smells of your cooking will be the best aroma for your guests.

- Keep appetizers for your dinner party light. You don't want to spoil your guests' appetites before the main event! Offer rice crackers and small slices of cheese. Or serve shrimp cocktail. One or two of these will leave plenty of room for dinner.

- Schedule time to turn on the music, light the candles, and relax before your guests arrive. Take off your apron, put your feet up, and take in the pretty table and your clean, comfortable room. Enjoy the aromas coming from the kitchen.

- Use your fireplace when guests come over. It makes a warm, instant welcome and a feeling of being at home.

Sesame Peanut Chicken Dip

*The unique flavor combinations of this dip will have people guessing
and coming back for more. It makes enough for a large crowd.*

2 tablespoons soy sauce
4 teaspoons sesame oil
2 cloves garlic, minced
4 cups shredded cooked chicken breast
3 (8 ounce) packages cream cheese,
  softened
8 green onions, thinly sliced

½ cup salted peanuts, chopped
2 cups fresh baby spinach, chopped
2 tablespoons sesame seeds
1 tablespoon fresh cilantro, finely
  chopped
1 (10 ounce) jar sweet and sour sauce
Crackers

In large resealable bag, combine soy sauce, sesame oil, and garlic; add chicken.
Seal bag and turn to coat; refrigerate at least 1 hour. Spread cream cheese onto

large serving platter; top with chicken mixture. Sprinkle with onions, peanuts, spinach, sesame seeds, and cilantro. Drizzle with sweet and sour sauce. Cover and refrigerate for at least 2 hours. Serve with your choice of crackers.

Notes

Hot Crab Dip

1 (8 ounce) package cream cheese, softened
8 ounces fresh crabmeat, picked over
⅓ cup mayonnaise
2 tablespoons onion, finely chopped
1 tablespoon whole milk
¼ teaspoon garlic salt
1½ teaspoons prepared white horseradish, or to taste
Crudités for serving (such as baby carrots, cucumber spears, cherry tomatoes, broccoli florets, radishes)

....

Place oven rack 6 inches from broiler and preheat oven to 350 degrees. In large bowl, beat cream cheese until smooth; add crabmeat, mayonnaise, onion, milk, garlic salt, and horseradish. Mix until well blended. Transfer to shallow 2½- to 3-cup ceramic baking dish and spread evenly. Bake 25 minutes or until browned around the edges. Broil 1 to 2 minutes or until top is golden brown.

Notes

Holiday Meatballs

Great as an appetizer but just as good served over rice as a main dish.

MEATBALLS:
2 pounds lean ground beef
1 cup cornflake crumbs
⅓ cup parsley flakes
2 eggs
2 tablespoons soy sauce
¼ teaspoon pepper
½ teaspoon garlic powder
⅓ cup ketchup
2 tablespoons onion, minced

SAUCE:
1 (16 ounce) can cranberry sauce
1 (12 ounce) bottle chili sauce
2 tablespoons brown sugar
1 tablespoon lemon juice

MEATBALLS: In large mixing bowl, combine all ingredients for meatballs; mix well. Roll into walnut-sized balls and arrange in greased 9x13-inch baking dish. SAUCE: In medium saucepan, combine ingredients for sauce. Cook sauce over medium heat until smooth and cranberry sauce is melted. Pour sauce over meatballs and bake uncovered at 350 degrees for 30 to 40 minutes.

Notes

Tortilla Pinwheels

The pinwheel design and flavor combo makes these disappear very quickly.

FILLING:
8 ounces sour cream
1 (8 ounce) package cream cheese,
    softened
1 (4 ounce) can diced green chilies,
    well drained
1 (4 ounce) can chopped black olives,
    well drained
1 cup cheddar cheese, grated
½ cup green onions, chopped
Garlic powder and seasoned salt to taste

TORTILLAS:
5 (10 inch) flour tortillas
Salsa
Fresh parsley or cilantro

FILLING: In medium mixing bowl, combine all filling ingredients together thoroughly. TORTILLAS: Divide filling and spread evenly over tortillas; starting at one end, roll tortillas. Cover tightly with plastic wrap, twisting ends. Refrigerate for several hours. Unwrap; cut in slices ½ to ¾ inches thick. Discard ends. Lay pinwheels flat on glass serving plate, leaving space in the center for a small bowl of salsa, if desired. Garnish with fresh parsley or cilantro.

Notes

....

....

....

Munchy Crunchy Party Mix

This is a basic version of a well-loved snack.
You won't want to stop once you start.

1 cup butter
3 tablespoons Worcestershire sauce
½ teaspoon garlic powder
2 drops hot pepper sauce
5 cups pretzel sticks

4 cups round toasted oat cereal
4 cups rice square cereal
4 cups wheat square cereal
3 cups mixed nuts

Heat and stir butter, Worcestershire sauce, garlic powder, and hot pepper sauce until butter melts. In large roasting pan, combine pretzels, cereals, and nuts. Drizzle butter mixture over cereal mixture; toss to coat. Bake at 300 degrees for 45 minutes, stirring every 15 minutes. Spread on foil; cool. Store mix in an airtight container.

Notes

White Chocolate Party Mix

A great gift idea.

16 cups popped popcorn
3 cups frosted round toasted oat cereal
1½ cups pecan halves
1 (14 ounce) package milk chocolate
  coated candy

1 (10 ounce) bag pretzel sticks
1 (10 ounce) package English toffee bits
2 (10 to 12 ounce) packages white
  chocolate chips
2 tablespoons vegetable oil

In large bowl, combine first six ingredients. In microwave or heavy saucepan, melt chips; add oil, stirring until smooth. Pour over popcorn mixture and toss to coat. Immediately spread onto two baking sheets; let stand until dry, about 2 hours. Store in an airtight container.

Notes

Holiday Brie en Croute

This pastry-covered brie makes an elegant and delicious appetizer.

Half of 17.3-ounce package of
   puff pastry sheets
½ cup orange juice
⅓ cup dried cranberries
1 egg
1 tablespoon water

½ cup apricot preserves or raspberry jam
¼ cup almonds, toasted and sliced
1 (13.2 ounce) round brie cheese
Crackers
Sliced apples

Thaw pastry sheets at room temperature for 30 minutes. In small saucepan, heat orange juice until warm. Remove from heat and stir in dried cranberries. Set aside. In small bowl, whisk egg and water. Unfold pastry sheets on lightly floured surface. Roll pastry into 14-inch square. Cut off corners to make a circle. Spread preserves to within an inch of the pastry edge. Drain cranberries and pat them dry with paper towel. Sprinkle cranberries and almonds over preserves. Top with cheese. Brush edge of circle with egg mixture. Fold two opposite sides over cheese. Trim remaining two sides to 2 inches from edge of cheese. Fold these two sides onto the round. Press edges to seal. Place seam side down on parchment-covered baking sheet. Decorate top with pastry scraps if desired. Brush with egg mixture. Bake at 400 degrees for 20 minutes or until golden brown. Let stand 1 hour. Serve with crackers and sliced apples.

Notes

Rueben Sauerkraut Balls

Reminiscent of a popular sandwich, these kraut balls are sure to please.

3 tablespoons unsalted butter
1 onion, finely chopped
1 cup finely chopped cooked ham
1 cup finely chopped corned beef
½ clove garlic, crushed
6 tablespoons flour
2 cups sauerkraut, drained and minced

2 teaspoons chopped fresh parsley
½ cup beef broth
1 quart oil for frying
1 egg
2 cups milk
2½ cups flour
4 cups fine dry bread crumbs

In large skillet, melt butter over medium-low heat. Add onion and cook
until softened. Stir in ham, corned beef, and garlic. Cook mixture, stirring

constantly for 1 minute. Stir in 6 tablespoons flour and cook mixture over moderate heat, stirring occasionally, for 3 minutes. Stir in sauerkraut, parsley, and broth; cook for 3 minutes or until thickened and pastelike. Spread mixture on platter and chill for at least 3 hours. Heat oil in deep fryer to 375 degrees. In bowl, whisk together egg, milk, and 2½ cups flour. Shape sauerkraut mixture by level teaspoons into balls, dip them into egg mixture, and roll them in bread crumbs. Fry balls in batches for 2 to 3 minutes or until golden brown. Transfer to paper towels to drain. Serve warm with Thousand Island dressing for dipping.

Bacon Cheese Stuffed Mushrooms

*Make these ahead of time and fill them when
you're ready to bake them. It saves on last-minute preparation.*

24 whole fresh mushrooms
  (smaller sized)
1 tablespoon olive oil
1 tablespoon minced garlic
1 (8 ounce) package cream cheese,
  softened
¼ cup grated parmesan cheese

¼ teaspoon ground black pepper
¼ teaspoon onion powder
¼ teaspoon ground cayenne pepper
3 strips bacon, fried and finely crumbled
  parmesan cheese
2 tablespoons butter, melted

Clean mushrooms with damp paper towel. Carefully break off stems. Chop stems extremely fine, discarding tough end of stems. Heat oil in a large skillet over medium heat; add garlic and chopped mushroom stems to skillet. Fry until any moisture has disappeared, taking care not to burn garlic. Set aside to cool. When garlic and mushroom mixture is no longer hot, stir in cream cheese, ¼ cup parmesan cheese, black pepper, onion powder, cayenne pepper, and bacon. Mixture should be very thick. Place filling in heavy resealable bag and snip off one end; fill mushrooms like a pastry. Sprinkle with additional parmesan cheese and drizzle with melted butter. Arrange mushroom caps on greased cookie sheet. It also works well to place mushrooms in nonstick mini muffin pan. Bake at 350 degrees for 20 minutes, or until mushrooms are piping hot and liquid starts to form under caps.

Yummy Cheese Fondue

Serve this delicious fondue with french bread cubes and vegetables.

1 cup dry white wine
½ teaspoon fresh lemon juice
1 clove garlic, minced
½ pound shredded swiss cheese

½ pound shredded gruyère cheese
2 tablespoons flour
¼ teaspoon salt
¼ teaspoon ground nutmeg

Mix wine, lemon juice, and garlic in cheese fondue pot or slow cooker; simmer. Place cheeses in resealable bag; add flour. Shake until cheese is coated. Add cheese mixture to wine, a small amount at a time. Stir after each addition of cheese until melted. When cheese has melted, stir in salt and nutmeg. Serve with cut-up french bread, broccoli, cauliflower, apples, and carrots.

Notes

Pear and Mushroom Strudel

½ cup butter, divided
1 cup finely chopped mushrooms
1 small onion, finely chopped
2 small pears, peeled and thinly sliced
¾ cup shredded gruyère or swiss cheese
⅓ cup sliced almonds

1 tablespoon stone-ground mustard
½ teaspoon salt
¼ teaspoon pepper
10 (9x14 inch) sheets phyllo dough
⅓ cup grated parmesan cheese, divided

In large skillet, heat 2 tablespoons butter; cook mushrooms and onion until tender. Stir in pears; cook 3 minutes longer. Remove from heat; stir in cheese, almonds, mustard, salt, and pepper. Cool to room temperature. Melt remaining butter. Place one sheet of phyllo dough on work surface; brush evenly with butter. (Keep remaining phyllo dough covered with plastic wrap and a damp towel to prevent it from drying out.) Sprinkle with 1½ teaspoons parmesan cheese. Layer with four more sheets of phyllo, brushing each sheet with butter and sprinkling with cheese. Spread half of pear mixture in 2-inch strip along short side of dough. Roll up jelly-roll style, starting with pear side; pinch seams to seal. Brush with butter. Transfer to parchment paper–lined 10x15-inch baking pan. Repeat with remaining phyllo, butter, parmesan cheese, and pear mixture. Bake at 375 degrees for 16 to 20 minutes or until golden brown. Cool for 5 minutes. Cut each strudel into 12 slices.

Notes

Warm Savory Cheese Dip

1 (8 ounce) package cream cheese, softened
2 cups mayonnaise
2 cups shredded cheddar cheese
1 large onion, finely chopped
8 bacon strips, cooked and crumbled
½ cup sweet red pepper, finely chopped
½ cup green pepper, finely chopped
1 teaspoon dried oregano
½ teaspoon garlic powder
2 drops hot sauce
1 round loaf (1 pound) sourdough bread
Assorted crackers

In large bowl, beat cream cheese until smooth and creamy. Add mayonnaise, cheddar cheese, onion, bacon, red pepper, green pepper, oregano, garlic powder, and hot sauce. Mix well. Cut the top fourth off loaf of bread; carefully hollow out bottom, leaving a 1-inch shell. Cut removed bread into cubes. Spoon cheese mixture into bread shell. Wrap shell in heavy-duty foil. Bake filled bread at 350 degrees for 1 hour or until heated through. Serve with bread cubes and crackers.

Notes

Spinach Cheese Balls

1 (9 ounce) box frozen spinach
1 large egg, slightly beaten
1 cup parmesan cheese, shredded
1 cup mozzarella cheese, shredded
1 teaspoon salt
1 teaspoon onion powder
1 teaspoon garlic powder
1 teaspoon dried oregano leaves

½ cup sour cream
2 tablespoons olive oil
1 (15 ounce) container ricotta cheese
2 cups flour
Vegetable oil, for deep-frying
¾ cup Italian-style bread crumbs
1 (25.5 ounce) jar pasta sauce, heated

Remove frozen spinach from pouch; place in colander. Thaw at room temperature or rinse with warm water until thawed; drain well. Squeeze spinach dry with paper towel. Mix egg, cheeses, salt, onion powder, garlic powder, oregano, sour cream, oil, and ricotta cheese in large bowl until well blended. Add spinach to cheese mixture; mix well. Stir in flour, 1 cup at a time, until well blended. Fill 10-inch skillet half full with oil; heat over medium heat until candy/deep-fry thermometer reads 350 degrees (or use deep fryer, add oil to fill line and heat to 350 degrees). Place bread crumbs in small bowl. Shape spinach-cheese mixture into 1½-inch balls (about 40), using about 1½ tablespoons for each; roll in bread crumbs and place on cookie sheet. Fry 6 balls at a time for 4 to 6 minutes, turning as necessary, until golden brown. With slotted spoon, remove balls from skillet; place on paper towels to drain. Cool 2 minutes before serving; serve with warm pasta sauce for dipping.

Pumpkin Black Bean Soup

3 (15 ounce) cans black beans,
   rinsed and drained
1 (16 ounce) can diced tomatoes
¼ cup butter
1¼ cups chopped onion
4 cloves garlic, chopped
1 teaspoon salt
½ teaspoon ground black pepper
4 cups beef broth

1 (15 ounce) can pumpkin puree
1 teaspoon cumin
½ teaspoon coriander
1 bay leaf
⅛ teaspoon cayenne pepper
3 tablespoons sherry vinegar
½ pound cooked ham, cubed
Sour cream, optional
Toasted pumpkin seeds, optional

Pour 2 cans black beans into food processor or blender, along with tomatoes.
Puree until smooth. Set aside. Melt butter in soup pot over medium heat.
  Add onion and garlic, and season with salt and pepper. Sauté until onion

is softened. Stir in bean puree, remaining can of beans, beef broth, pumpkin puree, cumin, coriander, bay leaf, cayenne pepper, and sherry vinegar. Mix until well blended; simmer for about 25 minutes or until thick enough to coat back of metal spoon. Stir in ham and heat through. Remove bay leaf before serving. Serve topped with a dollop of sour cream and sprinkle with toasted pumpkin seeds, if desired.

Notes

....

....

....

French Onion Soup

*Great as an appetizer, but it also makes a
tasty wintertime meal served with a salad.*

4 tablespoons butter
1 teaspoon salt
2 large red onions, thinly sliced
2 large sweet onions, thinly sliced
1 (14 fluid ounce) can chicken broth
1 (48 ounce) can beef stock
½ cup red wine
1 tablespoon Worcestershire sauce
2 sprigs fresh parsley
1 sprig fresh thyme leaves

1 bay leaf
1 tablespoon balsamic vinegar
Salt and freshly ground black pepper
to taste
4 thick slices french or italian bread
4 slices gruyère or swiss cheese slices,
room temperature
½ cup shredded asiago or mozzarella
cheese, room temperature

Melt butter in a large pot over medium-high heat. Stir in salt, red onions, and sweet onions. Cook 35 minutes, stirring frequently, until onions are caramelized and almost syrupy. Mix chicken broth, beef stock, red wine, and Worcestershire sauce in pot. Bundle the parsley, thyme, and bay leaf with twine and place in pot. Simmer over medium heat for 20 minutes, stirring occasionally. Remove and discard herbs. Reduce heat to low, mix in vinegar, and season with salt and pepper. Cover and keep over low heat to stay hot while you prepare the bread. Preheat oven broiler. Arrange bread slices on baking sheet and broil 3 minutes, turning once, until well toasted on both sides. Remove from heat; do not turn off broiler. Arrange 4 large oven-safe bowls or crocks on a rimmed baking sheet. Fill each bowl two-thirds full with hot soup. Top each bowl with 1 slice toasted bread, 1 slice cheese, and ¼ of the shredded cheese. Broil 5 minutes, or until bubbly and golden brown. Serve immediately.

Make Yourself at Home:
Tips and Tricks for the Hostess

Whether you're an entertaining novice or a party-throwing veteran, inviting people into your home can be a stressful and joyous time all wrapped into one. Take a deep breath and relax—nobody wants you to be wound so tightly that you aren't able to enjoy this special time with family and friends. And get-togethers during the holiday season have an even more special, eternal reason as you celebrate the birth of a baby that is the reason for our hope. That truth helps keep everything in perspective. Happy entertaining!

Now let us all with gladsome cheer
Go with the shepherds and draw near
To see the precious gift of God,
Who hath His own dear Son bestowed.

MARTIN LUTHER

And she brought forth her firstborn son,
and wrapped him in swaddling clothes,
and laid him in a manger.
LUKE 2:7

Before the Guests Arrive

- The busiest day ahead of any holiday gathering is not the day of, but the day before! Do all of your cleaning and shopping one or two days out, and prepare anything you can make ahead the day before. Keep your schedule clear of all but last-minute projects on the day of your party.

- Wear an apron whenever you are in the kitchen after you dress for company. One little splash or mishap can ruin your outfit—and your timing—if you have to change clothes.

- Put long hair up in a bun or ponytail when you're preparing food. You will be much more comfortable, and you'll lessen the possibility of a stray strand ending up in your guests' food.

- When planning a dinner party, set up your coffee and tea service ahead of time. Get out the service pieces you'll need for sugar and cream, and have dessert dishes and extra utensils ready to go on when dinnerware is cleared.

- Stick to tried-and-true recipes when entertaining. Your guests are not guinea pigs! Making a dish for the first time creates tension for you, and with the other normal stresses of entertaining, you don't need to worry about how a first attempt will turn out.

A "Scrambled" Dinner Party

Invite about eight friends over for a casual dinner. Assign each couple one side dish recipe you plan to serve (enough for each guest to have a small serving). That's all they need to know. The host provides an entrée and dessert, but your guests won't have any idea what you're serving or what anyone else is bringing.

The night of the party, there are no place settings; the only items for each guest are a menu and a pen. Create the menus by folding paper in half like a greeting card. When opened, the left side of the menu will be a list of every item on the menu (including eating utensils, each individual dish, and beverage), but each will be cleverly disguised under a new name. Mashed potatoes become "Clouds over Bethlehem," and a butter knife is "Herod's

Scepter." If your main dish is beef, you might call it "Cattle Are Lowing," a napkin is "Swaddling Clothes," and so on—pull out all your creative genius for this! The right side of the menu contains blank lines under the headings of COURSE I, COURSE II, COURSE III, one line for each item they'll be served from the left side of the menu. Have guests fill out all three courses at once, then write their names at the top and turn them in to servers.

You will need help in the kitchen for this event, so ask a few of the members of the church youth group to come help out for this fun evening. They will be filling orders, serving, and clearing after each course. (Forget the good china and use fun holiday paper products and plastic utensils for quick cleanup.)

The fun really starts when Course I appears: Someone gets a vegetable, dessert, and meat but didn't order a fork, so she only has a toothpick to eat it with! Someone else has unwittingly ordered a napkin, a glass of water, and all his silverware for Course I and has to eat his next two courses with his fingers!

When the meal is over, invite guests to finish off any of the food, drink, and dessert left in the kitchen, this time filling their own plates.

Guests' Arrival

- Nothing is so welcoming as the sight of you standing out on your porch when first-time guests come to your home. They will be straining to see house numbers and identify landmarks you've given them, but seeing you smiling and waving them in is a wonderful welcome.

- Make sure to have good lighting outside where guests are parking and entering your home. Steps can be tricky in the dark. Make sure your porch has been cleared of snow and ice.

- Avoid rushing your guests to the dinner table. Let your dinner finish cooking or keep it warm while you relax over drinks and appetizers with your guests. This puts the focus on them rather than the meal. When conversation is flowing, slip out to get ready to serve, and only then invite everyone into the dining room.

- Choose holiday music that will match the tone of your get-together. For sit-down dinners, play soft instrumental carols. For a more casual family affair, classic pop renditions of holiday songs might be a better option. And if there are kids in attendance, it's always fun to have some music that they can sing along to—especially split-track kids' albums.

Christmas Tea

Here's a fun idea for a holiday tradition: an old-fashioned Christmas tea. Send out invitations on cards with warm Christmas themes. Assign each guest a cookie or candy recipe found in this section (be sure to include the recipe in the invitation). Ask guests to bring the finished product on a pretty Christmas plate or glass pedestal cake holder for presentation.

Tea is usually held midafternoon with very light refreshments. Serve crustless finger sandwiches and a tray of fresh vegetables along with the candies and cookies. Place plates of food and treats all along the table and invite guests to serve themselves. Brew a few tea options and be sure to have a caffeine-free or herbal variety available. No tea bags allowed!

If you don't already own them, borrow a pretty selection of teapots, cream and sugar vessels, teaspoons, and small plates. An eclectic presentation of teacups and saucers is beautiful and fun, but few of us keep this kind of collection, so borrow pretty sets from friends.

If you wish, and if time allows, ask one of your guests who has agreed in advance, to demonstrate a simple take on an intimidating candy recipe, such as fudge. This activity is a fun conclusion to tea and can be a big encouragement to candy-making novices. Keep the demonstration to 20 or 30 minutes at the most.

Other tips:

- Be sure to return all borrowed china, cleaned and well packed, within a day or two of your event.

- Serve real cream, sugar, and sliced lemons with tea. Old-fashioned sugar cubes are fun, too.

- Let each guest take home a selection of cookies and candy as a favor. Have Christmas storage bags available if needed.

The Meal

- An easy way to make a dinner more festive is to serve drinks in fancy glasses. The fancier, the better. Pinkies up!

- Avoid overwhelming your dinner guests with huge portions. Start with a small amount and always offer seconds.

- Simple entertaining may include paper plates and cups now and again when big groups are expected and the menu is very simple and light. Just make sure to buy a sturdy brand or double-plate the cheaper kind.

- Some meals include buffet-line serving. Set the table with napkins and utensils only. Stack plates and drinking glasses near food and drinks for self-service. If the in and out of a large group at the table is too congested or disruptive, pass dishes around family style. Be sure to space little children between helpful adults.

- Keep water flowing. A good hostess keeps her eye on water glasses and fills them when they get low. A bowl of ice set out on the table is a good idea as well.

Happy Birthday, Jesus!

Hold a kids-only birthday party for Jesus. Invite as many as you can handle, and make sure you have enough adult help. Ask each child to bring along a baked Christmas dessert in a disposable container that will be taken to a local retirement center. Make or buy a large Christmas greeting card on which every child can sign, draw a picture, or write a message to the residents at the retirement center.

Decorate for Jesus' birthday with balloons, streamers, party hats, noisemakers, and party plates and napkins. Bake a cake and add as many candles as there are kids at the party. Remind children that Jesus' birth made it possible for us to be reborn! Then gather the kids around to sing "Happy

Birthday" to Jesus and blow out the candles together and enjoy cake and ice cream.

A nativity scene makes an excellent centerpiece for this party. Read a short, modern version of the Christmas story while the kids are seated.

Play Christmas-themed games.

As the party comes to a close, join hands in a circle and sing a Christmas carol or other seasonal song together. Children love to sing!

> The merry family gatherings—the old, the very young;
> the strangely lovely way they harmonize in carols sung.
> For Christmas is tradition time—traditions that recall
> the precious memories down the years, the sameness of them all.
>
> HELEN LOWRIE MARSHALL

Entertaining Décor

- A variety of short, fat, skinny, and uniquely colored candles makes a pretty glow for entertaining at the table. Set three or four candles on a small plate together. Arrange two plates and place them on either side of a bowl filled with colorful Christmas bulbs.

- Decorate with fresh evergreen boughs you trimmed from your Christmas tree before you put it up. After you trim them off, just store them on the back porch until you're ready for them. Pine is beautiful and fresh and looks elegant when placed around a candle's soft glow on the table or mantel.

- Drape festive, soft throws over sofas and armchairs. Guests love pulling them onto their laps if they get chilly.

- Don't hesitate to rearrange furniture a bit when having guests in. Try to create a comfortable setting for easy conversation. Bring in an extra easy chair and ottoman from another room, and clear end and coffee tables for serving desserts or setting drinks on.

- Modern sofas and armchairs are usually too crowded with decorative pillows for comfortable guest seating. Remove at least half beforehand, or place them on the floor next to the couch so your guest won't feel like she is undecorating your living room to find a seat.

HOLIDAY DECORATING

Pinecones and Berries

Pinecones and berries on a platter or bowl make a beautiful and inexpensive decoration. Find pinecones outdoors and use cranberries, or purchase artificial berries at a hobby store.

KID TIP: Allow kids to hunt for pinecones outside or at a local park. After you have picked out the nice ones to use indoors as decoration, allow children to decorate the remaining pinecones for the birds. Add peanut butter and sprinkle with birdseed and berries. Tie with red and green ribbon and attach to the trees and bushes outside.

Bead Garlands

Garlands aren't just for Christmas trees. Think outside the tree! Arrange red and silver bead garlands in bowls and vases and allow them to cascade over the edges. Setting the bowls on top of mirrors adds extra sparkle. Garlands look great on tables, mantels, countertops, staircases, etc.

Kid Tip: Kids can make their own garlands out of red and green paper. Cut strips of construction paper and attach with a glue stick. Make a special "countdown to Christmas" garland while you're at it. Start with one link on December 1st. Add a new paper link every day until Christmas. Write a special prayer or scripture on each link before you glue it together.

Cookie Recipe Favors

Here's a simple party favor that is sure to bring a smile to your guests' faces. Everyone loves the fun and festive shapes of cutout cookies!

ITEMS NEEDED:
3x5-inch index cards
Colorful ink
Cookie cutters

Hole punch
Ribbon

Write out your favorite Christmas cutout cookie recipe with colored pens. Or if you are having a large number of guests, print recipes from your computer and attach to recipe cards with glue or clear tape. Punch a hole in each recipe card and attach a cookie cutter with a colorful ribbon to give to each guest as a party favor. For an added personal touch, visit a kitchen store and pick out unique cookie-cutter shapes for each guest, based on his or her interests. For example, give a dog lover a dog bone–shaped cutter. For a musical person, give a music note-shaped cutter.

Notes

Gingerbread Bundt Cake Mix

Jar mixes are wonderful favors to send home with your guests.
Here's a Bundt twist on a traditional gingerbread.

1 cup sugar
2 cups all-purpose flour
1 cup whole wheat flour
2 teaspoons baking soda

2 teaspoons ground ginger
2 teaspoons ground cinnamon
1 teaspoon allspice
½ teaspoon cloves

In large bowl, combine all ingredients. Spoon mixture into 1-quart glass jar.
Attach recipe card with the following instructions (see back of this card).

Gingerbread Bundt Cake

1 cup molasses
1 cup butter, melted and cooled
3 ounces cream cheese, softened
3 eggs

Gingerbread Bundt Cake Mix
1¼ cups boiling water
Powdered sugar, optional

Preheat oven to 350 degrees. Grease and flour bundt pan. In large mixing bowl, combine molasses, butter, cream cheese, and eggs. Beat with electric mixer about 1 minute or until smooth. Add Gingerbread Bundt Cake Mix to the egg mixture alternately with the boiling water, beating on low speed until smooth. Pour batter into prepared pan. Bake for 40 to 50 minutes or until toothpick inserted near center comes out clean. Cool in pan on wire rack 15 minutes before inverting cake onto wire rack to cool completely. Place cake on serving plate and dust with powdered sugar, if desired.

Snowy Day Funnel Cake Mix

Here's a festive jar mix option that's fun for the whole family!

2 cups flour
3 tablespoons sugar
¼ teaspoon salt

1 teaspoon baking powder
1½ teaspoons baking soda

In medium bowl, combine all ingredients. Spoon mixture into 1-pint glass jar, tapping jar to settle if necessary. Attach recipe card with the following instructions (see back of this card).

Snowy Day Funnel Cakes

1 egg
¾ cup milk
Snowy Day Funnel Cake Mix

Oil for frying
Powdered sugar, optional

In medium bowl, combine egg and milk; beat well. Add Snowy Day Funnel Cake Mix and beat with spoon or whisk until mixture is smooth. In 10-inch skillet, pour oil to depth of 2 inches. Heat until hot but not smoking. Pour batter into funnel, holding finger over bottom hole. Hold funnel over skillet, removing finger. Move funnel, making circular designs to about 2 inches from side of skillet. When edges are brown, turn cake over and brown. Remove to paper towels. To serve, sprinkle with powdered sugar or top with chocolate sauce or fruit pie filling of choice.

Rich Chocolate Fudge Brownie Mix

*Send your guests home with this delicious
chocolate jar mix—everyone's favorite!*

2 cups flour
1 teaspoon baking soda
1 cup packed brown sugar

⅓ cup unsweetened cocoa powder
1 cup sugar
1½ cups semisweet chocolate chips

Combine flour and baking soda. Place in bottom of 1-quart glass jar. Layer
remaining ingredients in order given. Attach recipe card with the following
instructions (see back of this card).

Rich Chocolate Fudge Brownies

Rich Chocolate Fudge Brownie Mix
1 cup butter, softened
2 eggs

1 teaspoon vanilla
1½ cups buttermilk

Preheat oven to 400 degrees. Grease and flour 9x13-inch baking pan. In large mixing bowl, empty contents of Rich Chocolate Fudge Brownie Mix, stirring well to combine. Add butter, eggs, vanilla, and buttermilk. Beat until well blended. Spread batter into prepared pan. Bake for 35 to 40 minutes or until toothpick inserted near center comes out clean.

Blueberry Muffin Mix

Jar mixes are a fun, useful, and delicious favor to send home with your guests. These muffins make a great breakfast.

1¾ cups flour
½ cup sugar

2 teaspoons baking powder
1 teaspoon dried, grated lemon peel

In medium bowl, combine all ingredients. Spoon muffin mix into 1-pint glass jar. Attach recipe card with the following instructions (see back of this card).

Blueberry Muffins

Blueberry Muffin Mix
1 egg, slightly beaten
¾ cup milk

¼ cup vegetable oil
¾ cup fresh or frozen blueberries

Preheat oven to 400 degrees. Line muffin tin with paper baking cups. In large bowl, empty Blueberry Muffin Mix. Add egg, milk, and oil, stirring with a spoon until combined. Fold in blueberries. Pour batter into baking cups, filling two-thirds full. Bake for 20 minutes or until lightly golden. Remove muffins from tin to wire rack to cool slightly. Serve warm.